THINGS TO BUILD ON
POEMS OF CONSTRUCTIVE CHARACTER

| RESPECT | HONESTY | FORGIVENESS |

BY: GLORIA P. HUMPHREY

Print information available on the last page

Rev. date: 05/13/2015

To order additional copies of this book, contact:
Xlibris
1-888-795-4274
www.Xlibris.com
Orders@Xlibris.com

THINGS TO BUILD ON

POEMS OF CONSTRUCTIVE CHARACTER

Introduction

Hi I'm Hammer MC I will be assisting you with the content provided throughout this book. I know you're probably use to seeing me with a nail to hammer things down or build them up. But this time instead of a nail we will use poems to build up and hammer down character that will last a lifetime. Before we begin we need to prepare the surface to build, similar to a foundation of a house or tall building. Sometimes things are in the way that prevent a smooth base and require removal. Otherwise the building will lean and cause problems in the long run.

Building character begins with a heart that's clear, free from doubt and fear. Are you Ready?

Monsters In The Closet

First we must get rid
of the things that hide
Behind the door to a closet
locked from the inside
There's only one way
to open it and see
Every door has a master
unlocked by a key

Now the size of a monster
harry big and tall
Locked away over the years
from once very small
It's time for you to go
this house needs the space
Follow the exit sign
to a far far away place

Be careful not to let small things like a simple apology become the size of a monster

Respect

Our plans to build
now have a clean sleight
like every foundation
which stand up straight
When it comes to others
we must keep in mind
Although they're different
to treat them kind

Saying things that might
bring someone shame
pointing the finger
at another to blame
For some these things
are hard to forget
So try your best
to give everyone respect

Respecting others begins
by respecting yourself

Courage

Whenever you feel afraid
of a challenge you must face
don't turn and run away
there's a prize for the race
It may take hard work
so roll up your sleeve
If it's worth winning
then you must believe

The thing about courage
it starts in your mind
before you know it
you'll cross the finish line
Doesn't have to be a race
that you must win
Anything that seems hard
only needs you to begin

To face difficult things like a race or a test you just need a little courage

Honesty

There will come a time
you'll have a chance to cheat
a choice of yours alone
to sit in that seat
Asked a question which the
answer can be only one
If it's the truth then no
damage has been done

If you choose to lie
and it seems you got away
Sooner or later it will
catch up with you one day
Before you know it
liars will be your besty
separated from loyal
friends of honesty

Being honest is a quality
that follows you

George Washington 1732-1799
American General and The First President of the United States
"I cannot tell a lie"

Responsibility

Certain things are expected
at school and at home
like if you have a pet
by not letting it roam
Cleaning your room
and doing other chores
First things first
before going outdoors

Making sure to complete
your homework on time
Left undone will only
put you behind
A good habit to grow on
and life's simple key
being reliable is
a big responsibility

A responsible person is
one who is reliable

Sharing

Sometimes the things we do
involve us to take part
It makes a difference if we
do them from the heart
Then there are times we
really could care less
But that would only
make things a mess

If you notice someone
who looks to have a need
That's the perfect time
to do a good deed
It's always better to show
someone you care
especially if you have more
than enough to share

Whenever possible share with others that are in need

Forgiveness

Now this might be
the toughest of all
But the most important
If we're gonna build tall
When someone hurts you
without any regret
Sometimes it's not
as easy to forget

Or it may have been
an honest mistake
The kind that even a
best friend could make
But whichever one
you should address
It's always better to
find forgiveness

Forgiveness helps both the one whose to blame and the one who suffered the pain.

Thankful

Now the best way
to be polite
Is for your responses
to come out right
When given something
you didn't expect
A smile from your
heart should reflect

It's when we take this
virtue for granted
Like a weed choking
a flower planted
A pitiful state when
the heart becomes dull
The best place to be
is always thankful

Being thankful starts
in the heart

The End

Printed in the United States
By Bookmasters